They can't help it.

Mothers HAVE to say these things. It goes with the territory.

It's as though when a woman gives birth, she gets lots of flowers, tons of attention, and the solemn obligation to utter momilies.

How else to explain how universal these sentiments are? From generation to generation, mothers say the same things to their children.

Don't be mad. Be amused! They do it because they love you. But mostly because THEY JUST CAN'T HELP IT!!!

mother's Day 1985

From—
Lori

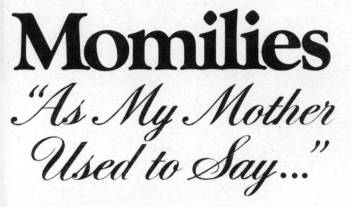

Momilies
"As My Mother Used to Say..."

MICHELE SLUNG

BALLANTINE BOOKS • NEW YORK

Library of Congress Catalog Card Number: 84-91788

ISBN 0-345-32289-4

Manufactured in the United States of America

First Edition: May 1985

For
My Mother

Dorothy Helen Miller Slung

Author's Note

Nothing seems to lodge in the mind so securely as the well-turned maternal phrase. Listen to your conversations and notice how frequently you offer up a maxim or a piece of advice that begins, "As my mother used to say..." Most children grow up and realize, at some rather wrenching moment, that Mom is fallible, maybe not even the smartest woman in the world, but by then it's too late—what she's said is what you've got.

Momilies get repeated from generation to generation, and sometimes the original meaning is lost, yet the sense remains. Many of them are all-purpose, a few are cruel, the majority loving; what's amazing is how, year in, year out, they guide our behavior, in ways both large and small. Momilies have no real geographic or class lines; they transcend most human divisions. All you need to do is think of one of your mother's favorite sayings and her voice is magically in your ear.

Whether you like it or not.

Mother Knows Best

I'm only doing this for your own good.

It's only your mother who's going to tell you the truth.

You only nag the ones you love.

As long as I'm around, I'll be your mother.

When my eyes close, yours will open.

꙳

You can be sure of two things in this world: there is a God, and your mother loves you.

Anna Hall Roosevelt

If somebody else's mother lets him jump off the Empire State Building, would you want me to let you do it, too?

Don't worry, there are plenty of fish in the sea.

A little of what you fancy does you good.

You can't be in twelve places with one behind.

You can't put one foot in two shoes at the same time.

You pays your money and you takes your choice.

If the French were so intelligent, they'd speak English.

In matters of taste, there is no disputing.

If your manners are perfect on the surface, you can be as unconventional as you wish, underneath.

Rebecca Rushall Friedman

When in doubt, write a thank-you note.

A bored person is a boring person.

All a little girl has to do is be amiable.

A playboy's nothing but a high-class bum.

A doctor's never the richest man in town, but he's always well-respected.

They've got orange peels on the slop pile—they must be rich.

Some folks make a dollar a day and spend a dollar a dime.

The best sleep is the sleep you get before midnight.

Nothing worthwhile happens after midnight.

You have to get up in the middle of the night to fool your mother.

Minna Schoenberg Marx

"Just You Wait..."

Be careful what you wish for; you might get it.

❧

Someday you boys are going to have to serve your country.

❧

Whistling girls and crowing hens always come to some bad end.

If I had talked to your grandmother the way you talk to me...

I suppose you think you're not going to be a parent one day too.

Amelia Keyser Stein

"I Mean Business"

I don't care if Jesus Christ himself is tap dancing on TV, turn it off and come to dinner this minute.

As long as you live under my roof, you'll do as I say.

I'm not asking you—I'm telling you.

That's not a request—it's an order.

Don't ask me *why*. The answer is *no*.

You don't have to like me, buster—I'm your mother.

Amalie Nathanson Freud

This is not a hotel.

Don't treat me like a kid—I'm your mother.

And don't come into my bedroom unless you're bleeding.

Louisa Van Velsor Whitman

"Go Ahead—Be Bad"

You must think rules are made to be broken.

If you're quiet, you must be up to no good.

You'll learn—pigs always get into trouble.

Doing bad was never in God's plan—if you blame Him, you're a fool.

Your ducks will come home to roost.

You have to have an answer for everything, don't you?

Lydia Beardsall Lawrence

Putting You In Your Place

Just because parents are allowed to do something doesn't mean kids get to do the same thing.

Everybody else may be doing it, but you're not going to.

Oh, so it's the egg teaching the chicken!

If you can't say anything nice, don't say anything at all.

He who toots his own horn never gets tooted.

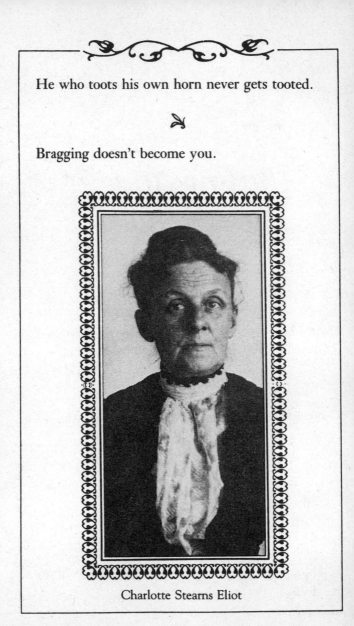

Bragging doesn't become you.

Charlotte Stearns Eliot

You're not the only pebble on the beach.

The sun doesn't rise and set around you.

Did you meet anyone today you liked better than yourself?

You won't be happy until you're crying.

So it's raining? You're not sugar—you won't melt.

You can dish it out, but you can't take it.

When your head swells up, your brain stops working.

Be a big wheel if you want—just remember that little dogs go to the bathroom on big wheels.

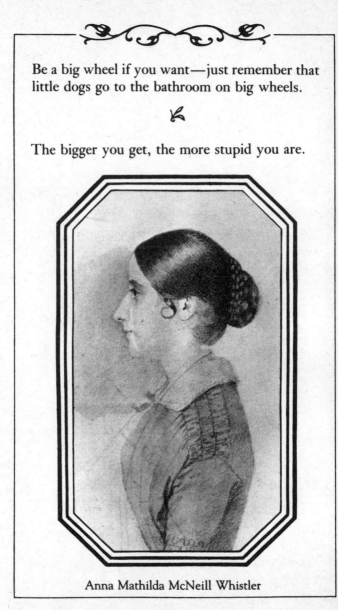

The bigger you get, the more stupid you are.

Anna Mathilda McNeill Whistler

Nobody likes a funny kid.

❧

You'll never be hung for your beauty.

❧

Fools' names, like fools' faces, are always seen in public places.

❧

Only two kinds of people complain of the cold: paupers and fools.

❧

Don't be so scared—if it doesn't have teeth, it won't bite you.

❧

Little animals don't eat big ones.

❧

Are you a man or a mouse?

❧

There's room for everyone at the table—except the Devil.

You've buttered your bed—now lie on it.

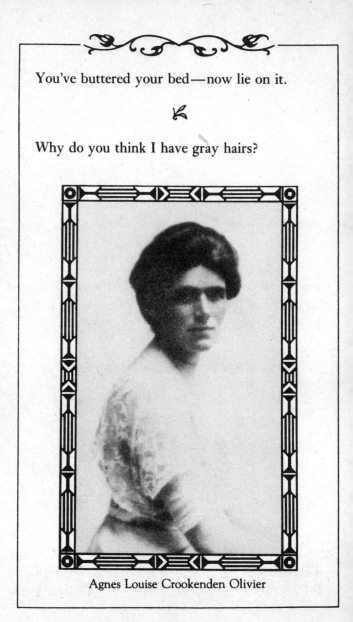

Why do you think I have gray hairs?

Agnes Louise Crookenden Olivier

The World Is A Dangerous Place

Remember the three B's: be careful, be good, and be home early.

Whenever you leave the house, put a dime in your shoe—in case you have to make a phone call.

Always give a penny to a poor old man—he may be Jesus in disguise testing you.

Never trust a man who wears a metal watchband.

I'd trust that man as far as I could sling a piano.

Never be in bed during a thunderstorm.

Grace Hall Hemingway

Never use the plumbing during a thunderstorm.

Sit in the middle of the living room during a thunderstorm.

Never drink out of a water fountain—you don't know who's been there before you.

Always put toilet paper on the seat.

Put that down! You don't know where it's been!

A dog always knows when you're afraid of it.

Don't take rides from strangers.

Don't take candy from strangers.

Don't go into dark alleys.

... And don't go near any cliffs.

Lela Owens McMath

"You'll Regret It"

Don't cross your eyes or they'll freeze that way.

If you swallow the stone, a cherry tree grows in your stomach.

If you swallow your gum, a horse will grow in your stomach.

Never nap after a meal or you'll get fat.

Don't put anything wet on the bed.

Don't lean back in the movies or you'll get ring-
worm.

Sara Warmbrodt Taylor

Don't run with a lollipop in your mouth.

If you go to bed with wet hair, you'll be gray before you're thirty.

Don't wear good underwear to the doctor or your bill will be higher.

Never learn how to iron a man's shirt or you'll wind up having to do it.

Don't sit too close to the television, it'll ruin your eyes.

Never try on anyone else's glasses or you'll go blind.

If you don't wash your hands after you go to the bathroom, it'll go to your brain.

Don't hit your mother or your hand will come out of your grave.

Anna Johnson LeSueur

Some Don'ts

Don't do anything you wouldn't do if I were sitting on your shoulder.

Don't start anything you don't plan to finish.

Don't let your emotions rule your head.

Don't say no without thinking twice.

Don't expect too much and you'll never be disappointed.

Don't expect from people what they're not capable of giving.

Hulda Minthorn Hoover

Don't bother to get angry at people who don't matter to you.

Don't let grass grow under your pencil—go ahead and do your homework.

Don't be a Philadelphia lawyer.

Don't say "drapes."

Don't sleep with the bedspread on the bed.

Don't put any beans up your nose.

Mildred Frances Cowan Turner

Running Away

Is that a threat or a promise?

If you leave, don't come back.

If you leave, it's easy to show me your back, but when you come back you have to show me your face.

Good, I'll pack your lunch.

Rosalie Mercurio DiMaggio

Mom Tries Sarcasm

Excuse me for living.

⤮

Don't say "she!" Who's "she?" The *cat's* mother?

⤮

Why don't you go out and play on the yellow line?

⤮

I can't shoot you—there's a law against it.

If you get separated from me in the crowd...
write.

If your ship doesn't come in, maybe your canoe
will.

Henrietta Trisch Willkie

"You Can Do It!"

If a thing is worth doing, it's worth doing well.

Everybody has to do the best with what he's got.

Everybody makes his own contribution.

Never say "never."

Show 'em greatness.

❧

He's no better than you—we all stand up naked inside our clothes.

Odessa Grady Clay

You're not in competition with anyone but yourself.

Anyone's a fool who doesn't try to live up to his dreams and abilities.

Every time you give up pleasure for duty, you're a stronger person.

Keep all strings a' drawing.

Don't dawdle—quick's the word and sharp's the action!

Aloise Steiner Buckley

Ladies And Gentlemen

A lady always has a clean handkerchief, gloves, and a hat.

A lady always has a handkerchief and pocket money.

A lady never uses a toothpick.

A lady never smokes on the street.

A lady doesn't swear aloud.

A skirt should be tight enough to show you're a woman, but loose enough to show you're a lady.

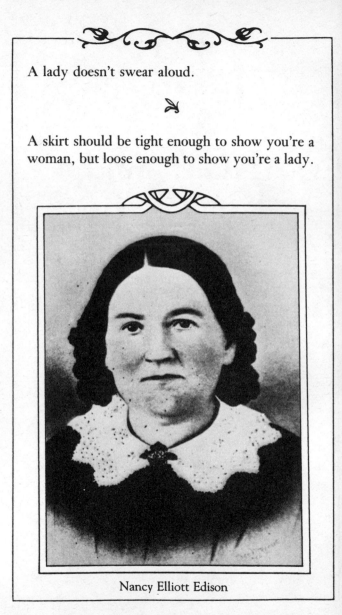

Nancy Elliott Edison

A lady never sits with her knees parted.

Horses sweat, men perspire, ladies glow.

Every house has to have at least one lady.

Call her a woman...we don't know if she's a lady.

"Gentlemen" is a word that gentlemen never use, but ladies sometimes have to.

A gentleman doesn't strike a lady.

Nice people don't put cream in their after-dinner coffee.

No one in our family would drink beer out of a can.

Josephine Lee Price

What You Wear

Always put on clean underwear in the morning, in case you're in an accident.

Go ahead and try it on—you can't compare yourself to a hanger.

Who's paying for all these clothes, anyway?

I didn't buy all these clothes just to decorate your closet.

Always buy one good dress instead of three cheap ones.

The important thing is to get a good bra.

Paula Stern Kissinger

Are you sure there's enough room in the crotch?

An extra half-inch at the end of your hem is like an extra half-inch at the end of your nose.

Your shoes should always be darker than your hemline.

Always wear your strings of pearls in odd numbers.

Always wear a coat and tie when you go on an airplane.

White is not a winter color.

Don't wear white until Easter or after Labor Day.

Blue and green should never be seen.

Brown is a neutral color.

Jeanne Weil Proust

Don't take off your sweaters before May.

Save your lace for your nighties.

Lovers shouldn't wear linen.

It's not what you wear; it's who you are.

Susan Tadd Graham

The Way You Look

If you want to be beautiful, you have to be willing to suffer a little.

You've got a face only a mother could love.

You'll never be a picture.

Pretty doesn't hurt.

If you carry yourself like a beauty, people will think of you as one.

First thing when you wake up in the morning, go to the mirror and smile.

Jennie Jerome Churchill

Get your hair out of your eyes.

Put some color in your cheeks.

Take off some of that lipstick—your mouth looks like a chicken's ass in pokeberry time.

Tan fat looks better than pale fat.

Don't worry—it's only baby fat.

Sit up straight.

Throw your shoulders back and you won't feel so cold.

Stick out your chest—here comes the iceman.

Clean your glasses—you can't be optimistic with a misty optic.

Georgie Drew Barrymore

Wash behind your ears or you'll have a potato field growing back there.

⚓

It's no disgrace to get head lice, but it is to keep them.

⚓

The only thing that counts in a job interview is clean fingernails.

⚓

Wash your elbows whenever you have the opportunity.

⚓

Put on hand lotion every time you think of it.

⚓

For every white hair you pluck out, two more will grow in.

⚓

Girls who pierce their ears are no better than they should be.

Nice girls don't wear ankle bracelets.

❧

Only sluts wear half-slips.

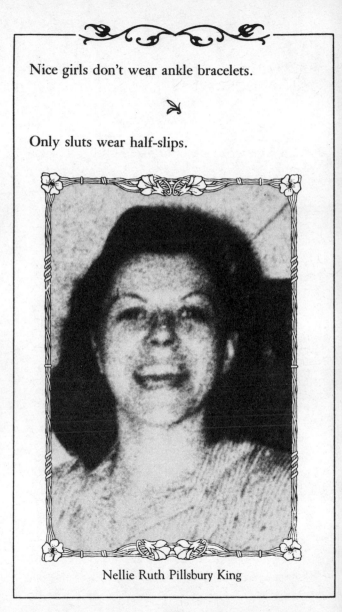

Nellie Ruth Pillsbury King

Around The House

How come you always offer to do the dishes at other people's houses?

❧

Here's how you help: first, you take the dishes off the table.

❧

It's just as easy to wash a dish well as it is to wash it badly.

❧

Always clean up in the kitchen as you go along.

Close the door behind you—were you born in a jail?

Never answer the phone on the first ring.

Sarah Morse Borden

I know if you clean up your room, it's bound to rain.

I don't see any hooks on that floor.

A drop of oil or a drop of spit works wonders.

Leave a dead fly and others gather.

Always put the zipper on the inside of a pillow case so you won't cut your face at night.

Sleep tight and don't let the bedbugs bite.

Wake up, snakes, and crawl! June bugs are hopping!

You have to make your bed in case the house burns.

How can you sleep in an unmade bed?

Polly Scobell Cartland

Foodstuff

Think of all the starving children in China (India, Armenia, etc.).

If you don't clean your plate, you won't get any dessert.

If you eat all your carrots, you'll be able to see in the dark.

Eat your fish—it's brain food.

All the vitamins are in the skin.

The crust is the best part of the bread.

Cynthia Stanton Baum

Eat the crusts of your bread so your hair will get nice and curly.

Ꮬ

When a date takes you out for dinner, never order chicken or spaghetti because there's no way to eat either neatly.

Ꮭ

Why do you want to order that out, when you can get it at home?

Ꮬ

Don't eat chocolate ice cream—it's made of left-over vanilla.

Ꮭ

Crabs and ice cream don't mix.

Ꮬ

I scream, you scream, we all scream for ice cream.

Ꮭ

Don't eat milk with tuna fish—you'll get hives.

Ꮬ

If you eat too many doughnuts, you'll turn into one.

If you don't eat your okra, you won't catch any fish.

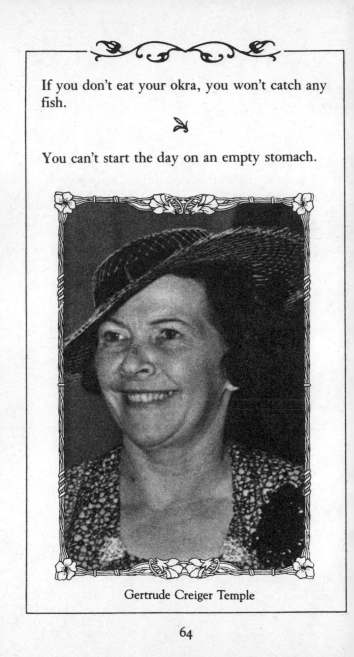

You can't start the day on an empty stomach.

Gertrude Creiger Temple

You can't read and digest at the same time.

Thirty-seven chews to a bite!

Chew your bananas.

Drink tea only out of a china teacup.

A good housewife always has lemons in her refrigerator.

It's a sin to put even bread crumbs on the fire.

If there's enough, put a crust on it; if there isn't, make it into soup.

The better the butter, the better the batter.

Cold food gives you a bellyache.

Don't turn up your nose!

It all winds up in the same place anyway.

Helen Lena Fritsche Cronkite

"Let Me Feel Your Forehead"

If it didn't taste bad, it wouldn't be medicine.

Don't go in the water for an hour after eating.

Don't go out of the house with your hair wet or you'll get a cold.

Sneakers ruin your feet.

The more you scratch it, the more it's going to itch.

It'll never get well if you pick it.

Adèle-Eugénie-Sidonie Landoy Colette

Don't stifle a sneeze.

Don't get someone else's breath, and you'll never get sick.

If any germ survives that, it's your friend.

The night air will make you sick.

Eat local honey—wherever you go—to avoid allergies.

If you have a head, you have headaches.

Margaret Majer Kelly

Love And Marriage

It's just as easy to fall in love with a rich man as a poor one.

Don't marry for money—marry where money is.

She who marries for money, earns it.

Throw yourself at a man's head and you'll land at his feet.

You don't have to marry every boy you go out with.

You don't want to chase a man and get him, because then he'll always remember how he was gotten.

Ella Quinlan O'Neill

Anyone who'd run away with you would drop you at the first lamppost.

If he tries to kiss you, call me.

Don't be such a smarty-pants—you'll scare the boys away.

You'll never get a boyfriend if you don't learn to play bridge.

Girls are like streetcars—there'll be another one along in ten minutes.

When you're on a date, order one drink and sip it slowly.

If you marry a gentile, he'll beat you and drink.

Don't marry anyone until you've seen them drunk.

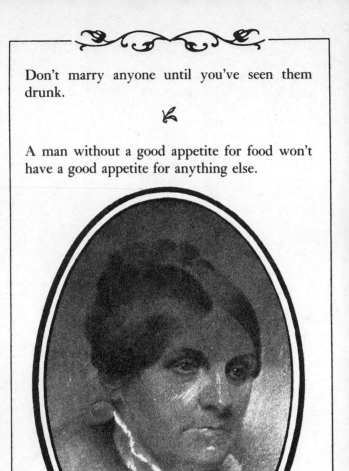

A man without a good appetite for food won't have a good appetite for anything else.

Abigail May Alcott

Save yourself for your husband.

Why should a farmer buy a cow when he can get the milk for free?

I knew he wasn't right for you, anyway.

What does his father do?

Pauline Koch Einstein

Relatively Speaking

No matter what happens, you'll always have your family.

You can choose your friends, but you can't choose your relatives.

I don't care whether you like them or not—you're related.

Treat your friends like family and your family like friends.

Wait 'til your brother cries for an hour before you give in.

If you can't get along with your brothers and sisters, how can you expect to get along with the world?

Ethel Milne Gumm

A Few
Superstitions

Wish on your eyelash and blow it away.

Lift up your legs when you go over a railroad track and make a wish.

Always eat the tip of a piece of pie last and make a wish on it.

Never start a trip on a Friday.

Never kill a spider—it'll bring bad luck.

Don't ever talk about the future and forget to say "God willing."

Frances Zuchowski Liberace

Proverbial
Wisdom

Two wrongs don't make a right.

The apple doesn't fall far from the tree.

Water seeks its own level.

A miss is as good as a mile.

Imitation is the sincerest form of flattery.

A fool and his money are soon parted.

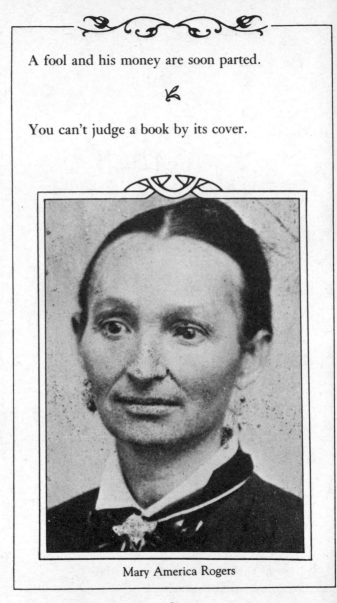

You can't judge a book by its cover.

Mary America Rogers

In the dark all cats are gray.

The way to a man's heart is through his stomach.

It's no use crying over spilt milk; there's enough water in it already.

Handsome is as handsome does.

You can't make a silk purse out of a sow's ear.

You catch more flies with honey than with vinegar.

Pride goes before a fall.

If wishes were horses, beggars would ride.

If my grandmother had wheels, she'd be an omnibus.

Little pitchers have big ears.

Silence is golden.

Margaret Isabella Balfour Stevenson

Acknowledgments

I'd like to thank all the friends and friends of friends who helped: Patrick Ahern, Deborah Amos, Marian Babson, Jane Barlow, Reid Beddow, Betty Bloch, Ron Bloch, Ellen Boyers, Amanda Burden, Maurice Braddell, Taylor Branch, Joan Brandt, Sam Brown, Art Buchwald, Elisabeth Bumiller, Jonathan Carroll, Diane Cleaver, Mary Lee Coffey, Barbara Cohen, Richard Cohen, Janet Coleman, Jan Deeb, Alice Digilio, Michael Dirda, Mary Ann Donovan, Susan Dooley, Jan Drews, Nancy Dutton, Gayle Engel, Garrett Epps, Nick Eskidge, Kitty Ferguson, Pie Friendly, Harriett Gilbert, Lynn Goldberg, Bonnie Goldstein, Judy Green, Linda Greider, Christina Hammond, Rick Hertzberg, Barbara Howson, Mary Jarrett, Martha Jewett, Kathy Jones, Betsy Kane, Leslie Kantor, Stan Kantor, Steve Kelman, Meg King, Nina King, Stephen King, Michael Kinsley, Michaela Kurz, Myla Lerner, Gail Lynch, Mark Lynch, Christy Macy, Evan Marshall, Judith Martin, Kathy Matthews, Triny McClintock, Patricia McGerr, Marilyn Mitchell, Gene-Gabriel Moore, Nancy Pepper, Susan Percy, Claudine Peyre, Terry Pristin, Dermot Purgavie, Sally Quinn, Eden Rafshoon, Jerry Rafshoon, Eleanor Randolph,

Coates Redmon, George Rider, Glenn Roberts, Paula Roberts, David Rubenstein, Wilfred Sheed, Victoria Sloan, Amanda Smith, Caron Smith, Margaret Stannek, Alison Teal, John Teal, Susan Teal, Tom Teal, Val Teal, George W.S. Trow, Judith Van Ingen, Lydia Viscardi, Nicholas von Hoffman, Elsa Walsh, Jim Weisman, Steve Weisman, Celeste Wesson, Marjorie Williams, Doug Winter, Millicent Woods, Bob Woodward, Emily Yoffe.

Special thanks, too, go to: Gene Barnes, Sallie Bingham, Victoria Haines, Michael Patrick Hearn, Margo Howard, Mona Joseph, Jim Lardner, Robert Phelps, Mildred Schwartz, Louis Sheaffer, Wendell Willkie II.

KEY TO PHOTOGRAPHS